50

WAYS YOU CAN

REACH THE WORLD

Tony Campolo
& Gordon Aeschliman

INTERVARSITY PRESS
DOWNERS GROVE, ILLINOIS 60515

InterVarsity Press® is the book-publishing division of InterVarsity Christian Fellowship®, a student movement active on campus at hundreds of universities, colleges and schools of nursing in the United States of America, and a member movement of the International Fellowship of Evangelical Students. For information about local and regional activities, write Public Relations Dept., InterVarsity Christian Fellowship, 6400 Schroeder Rd., P.O. Box 7895, Madison, WI 53707-7895.

All Scripture quotations, unless otherwise indicated, are taken from the HOLY BIBLE, NEW INTERNATIONAL VERSION. NIV®. Copyright ©1973, 1978, 1984 by International Bible Society. Used by permission of Zondervan Publishing House. All rights reserved.

Cover illustration: Paul Turnbaugh

ISBN 0-8308-1395-0

Printed in the United States of America ∞

Library of Congress Cataloging-in-Publication Data

Campolo, Anthony.
    50 ways you can reach the world/Anthony Campolo and Gordon
Aeschliman.
      p.   cm.
    ISBN 0-8308-1395-0
    1. Evangelistic work. 2. Witness bearing (Christianity)
I. Aeschliman, Gordon D., 1957-   II. Title.   III. Title: Fifty
ways you can reach the world.
BV3793.C35   1993
269'.2—dc20   93-26176
                                                                             CIP

15	14	13	12	11	10	9	8	7	6	5	4	3	2	1
04	03	02	01	00	99	98	97	96	95	94	93			

Restless
Heart

· · · · · · · · · · ·

We are not able to understand the love of God.
It is a mystery to us that the One who created the splendid schools of fluorescent coral-reef fish, the One who stretched the stars like a canopy over the earth and pushed the mountains up from the deep, the same One who scattered entire galaxies billions of years beyond our reach, is the One who woos us into his kingdom.

The images of God in the Scriptures include the Mother Hen who would gather us under her wing, the Lover who calls to us in the middle of the night to join him in the flower garden, the Servant who hangs on the splintered wood to bridge the gulf that separates us, the Warrior who gallops in on a white horse to rescue us in the final hour.

Who wouldn't feel loved by that passionate Person?

God is restless in his love for us. We are not some doctrinal project that waits for cosmic resolution, nor are we pieces of merchandise that fortunately made it into the bin marked "chosen." Nor do we merely serve as the battleground of a heavenly war with Satan and the diabolic host of demons.

We were conceived in love. All of us. And as a tender, perfect parent, God is pursuing us with untiring resolve. He will keep at it to the very end of time.

The Scriptures which portray God in those images of Mother, Lover, Servant and so on tell us of a complete love. God is wholesome in his mercy to the world. He heals the brokenhearted, forgives sins, feeds the hungry, shelters the homeless, visits the prisoner, liberates the oppressed, mourns with those who have lost their loves, restores energy to the weak.

We have benefited from that great love. But we are also the couriers of that great love. This is a mystery too! God allows each of us the high honor of representing his mercy and justice to a broken, brutalized world. We speak for the King. We are the hands and feet of the King. If that doesn't boggle your mind, you need some serious help.

This book is the last in our series on simple ways Christians can make a difference. This one focuses specifically on the global, righteousness-seeking, missionary heart of God. God is a missionary God, and therefore, as John Stott puts it, "we had *better* be a missionary people."

We hope you will find these fifty ideas helpful to you in your commitment to God's global work, starting right where you are. It is packed with ideas—some that will take as few as ten minutes, others that will require a whole lifetime. Be sure to check out the other four books in the 50 Ways series. Together they represent our understanding of the wholesome love of God for the world today.

Our hope for you (as for ourselves) is that as you read these ideas, God will give you grace to step forward into the pain of society and be people who bear the wounds of the world, both in your hearts and on your hands. May we love in both word and deed.

Yours for the world that waits . . .

Section
1

Lifestyle
· · · · · · · · · · · · · ·

1

Be a Friend

. . . .

We have discovered that one of the greatest barriers to reaching out to the world is the tendency to "programmize" the gospel. By this we mean the packaging of the good news into formal outreach schemes. This comes from a sincere desire to bring people into a personal relationship with Jesus Christ. We have no argument with that good goal. The problem is, these programs leave us with the idea that telling others about Christ is an unusual activity for Christians, that ministry is so unnatural that we have to receive special training to serve as salt and light in today's world.

We disagree. We believe that telling others about Jesus is as natural as breathing—because that is part of the physiology of being spiritual beings. We "take in" Jesus and we give him out. We cannot survive spiritually without this breathing. That is why our first suggestion in the book is so simple: Develop the art of being a friend. That's it.

Christians need to relax with the understanding that the good news is truly good news. Our friendships are the primary medium for passing it on. Sometimes we are tempted to embrace lofty, romantic notions of traveling to foreign places where we will share about Jesus. That's a trap. It's a trap because we are inferring that the gospel transfers more naturally in unfamiliar settings. We don't have to be nervous about breathing this special message of love! Jesus is our friend and delights in our sincere desire to bring others into the kingdom.

Begin with the circle of friends God has already brought into your life. There may be one or two persons who are a little closer to the center of that circle—friends who have already experienced the warmth of caring and honest exchange between the two of you. Ask God to open doors for communicating his life into these friendships. Don't wait to "spring the trap" on them! This isn't some kind of calculated hunt. Trust God for the wisdom to be more explicit with your faith at the right moments. Ultimately, it is the life you live that gives definition to the gospel. Your words are simply the translation.

If you believe God is calling you into crosscultural ministry, pastoral ministry at home or lay work in your own neighborhood and place of employment (and that pretty much covers all of us), the most important thing you will ever do is build genuine friendships.

2
Commit Yourself to Evangelism

Those of us who decide to become involved in the world, to see it touched by the love of Jesus, will discover that love takes many forms. Our actual daily activities could be as diverse as rebuilding airplane engines, opening mail, sewing up bodies and teaching students. Our commitments, whatever forms they take, are unified by a common call to live the life of Jesus as clearly as a light set on a hill. Our entire existence and purpose are derived from this Person.

Being committed to evangelism does several important things for us. First, it is a mooring point. It keeps us tethered to our roots. It prevents us from drifting into a sea of fuzzy thinking where Christ is demoted to one of several "options" for life. The commitment to verbally share the good news regularly brings our minds back into line with the experience of seeing God go to work for us; it keeps our minds tender with the memories of grace and forgiveness, of a broken heart repaired. And it reminds us of our personal history of faith in a world where reason is too often king.

Being committed to evangelism also serves to give us focus. The hard work of ministry can discourage us—broken computers, long hours, disgruntled staff, too many hungry people and financial stress all have a way of wearing on our enthusiasm for the kingdom. We can forget during these times that we are the privileged couriers of life, that we are God's hands and feet in a world that desperately waits to know its Creator. If we are actively seeking ways to share our faith, we are able to pull the sometimes tedious, overwhelming and draining work back into focus: Christ is our all!

And being committed to evangelism keeps us honest in our discipleship. We are not on a quest to become super-Christians—like some overdeveloped bodybuilder with all that muscle and no place to go. We are not on a spiritual quest to outdo others in the Great Commission. Rather, we are dependent on the kind and constant care of the One who invited us into the fold. We are being transformed by the renewing work of the Holy Spirit as we go about the business of making disciples of all nations. The work that Christ has been doing in us since the day of our salvation is the hope we carry for others who have yet to receive that gift.

We suggest that you link up with a couple of friends who want to be serious about the Great Commission and who have the urgent sense that evangelism must be a normal part of daily life. Commit to praying together for opportunities to share your faith with others. Pray that God will give you a love for sharing the good news. This can be a threatening step of faith, but it is a good one. Don't worry if you stumble along the way—be patient with the process. And report back to each other the ways in which God is honoring your prayers.

3
Stretch the Comfort Zones
· · · · · · · · · · ·

A commitment to cooperate with God's desire to win the whole world with his love is a decision to place ourselves in some new and unfamiliar circumstances.

We often resist these experiences. We much prefer sights, tastes, smells, customs and people that are "normal." The result of this tendency, of course, is that we become terribly boring people! All of our friends look like our second cousins. And our food looks as if it all came from the same mass-production center.

God is rich in diversity. All the earth speaks of a creative God who could not resist the adventure of going down new avenues of design and color. We are paupers for our resistance to this splendor. Somehow we need to be converted back to a sense of this miracle of diversity and put away the temptation to find security in sameness. We will discover that God has prepared for us a virtual banquet table of delicacies—and we'll wonder how we were able to be satisfied with a steady diet of just white bread. Clearly we were malnourished and misguided, but it was our fear of the unknown that kept us from the treat.

Being a part of God's desire to touch all the world is not only a wonderful gift to the people we engage; it is God's gift back to us as we rub against the new and exotic.

We are suggesting that you make it a part of your regular lifestyle to stretch those comfort zones. It is always good to include friends in new commitments, so single out two or three who are ready to explore with you. Decide on ways to bump against the unfamiliar. Here are a few possibilities:

☐ Choose three ethnic restaurants that are new to your experience. Each month go out to lunch with your friends to one of them. After a year of this you will have eaten out twelve times and you will have tried out several options at each place (four times at each restaurant). Or, if you live in a large metropolitan area, you will be able to try *twelve* different kinds of food in a year if you wish!

☐ Visit a neighborhood that is unlike yours. Take a stroll through the shopping district, business center and residential area. If there is a park, pack a lunch and surround yourself with people who very well may not speak your language.

☐ When shopping for regular household items and groceries,

choose a store that attracts clients other than your typical neighbors. Buy a few food items that are beyond your usual repertoire and go home to experiment with a couple of friends in preparing something new and (maybe) delicious.

In time you will discover that you are salivating for these new experiences. What once was a threat has now become a welcome friend. Then look for new ways to stretch those comfort zones.

4
Read Your Bible

· · · · · · · · · · · ·

Seriously, Bible reading is a good idea.

But how about adding a special focus?

We often miss some of the Bible's major story lines simply because we have not been trained to follow those golden threads that weave chapter to chapter, book to book. God's love for the world is the dominant story in Scripture, but we often overlook it for some of the minor themes. A group of peers at a Christian college on the West Coast had a good solution to this problem. They committed to study the Bible together for a full semester. Their plan was simple enough. They read on their own each day for a full hour. No in-depth studies—just a straight reading of the Bible beginning at Genesis. Anytime they bumped into a verse or collection of verses that gave a hint of God's compassionate nature, they highlighted that passage with a marker. Once a week they got together to discuss what new views they had gained on our compassionate Lord. The time ended with prayer for God to replicate that compassionate nature in their own hearts.

You can imagine what impression this kind of reading begins to make on the understanding of God's nature. As these students looked at the variety of needs about them and in the world and tried to apply compassion to them, their natural response became prayer and action. We think these students had a marvelous plan. The Bible came alive to them as did their world.

Our suggestion, then, follows on their example. Pick a group of friends who want to grow in their understanding of God's loving nature. Commit to a regular time of study and prayer—be sure to pick a reasonable schedule. Here are some possible variations on the theme:

☐ Do a word study on several related words—for example, *justice, righteousness* and *mercy*. Write down what circumstances in the Bible prompted God to action in these areas. Figure out what following God may mean today in this regard.

☐ As you read through the Scripture each week, also read the newspaper. When you are together as a group, pray through specific needs you read about in the paper, asking God to move you and others to be compassionate people in a hurting world. Specific situations help put a concrete nature to God's love.

☐ Choose a brief passage each week that you can memorize as

a group. This is a sure way to push God's nature deeper into your own nature.

By the way, that group of students liked the idea so much that they kept up their weekly routine until they had worked their way through the entire Bible.

5
Skip
Church
· · · · · · · · · · ·

Some pastors will object to this suggestion, no doubt.
But don't worry, we aren't suggesting this for every Sunday, just
a few Sundays a year.

There is a reason behind this suggestion! Christians are too
often taught to be suspicious of each other. The basis for this
really has very little to do with purely doctrinal issues. Who
knows all the causes for this (we can surmise a few), but we have
all experienced this phenomenon to some degree. This "training" leaves us fearful of venturing outside our home church
walls. We do not want to become "contaminated" in our doc-

trine and led away from Christ.

If we were to sit back and think how silly this narrow-minded thinking actually is, we would be a little embarrassed. There are consequences to this parochialism. The world does not see a witness of a church that fits Jesus' prayer: "May they be brought to complete unity to let the world know that you sent me" (Jn 17:23). Instead, the world sees petty fights and turns away. This haughty view of ourselves—for that is what it really is—also hurts efforts at discipling the nations for Christ. If we have trouble mixing with Christians in our own country, how much harder it will be to mix abroad. Differences in tradition are greatly magnified by culture.

Not only are efforts at evangelization hurt, but Westerners assume that Christians abroad need to be converted to their Western traditions. This is highly insulting to grown men and women of the faith who live in other nations. It smells very much like some of the historical problems the Third World has experienced when the powerful West has imposed its traditions and laws upon people of other cultures. The efforts of Western Christians become interpreted as a power play of "us vs. them" instead of deeds of service and love.

Okay, how does skipping church help this problem?

We suggest that on an occasional Sunday you attend another church in your town. The goal is to learn how another group of Christians expresses love and obedience for Jesus Christ. Pick a church that is quite different from your own, and be careful not to show up sniffing for problems in their beliefs. It may help to choose a church attended by a friend.

If you want to take the idea a little further, we recommend

that you become a regular member of another church's weekly Bible study meeting or prayer meeting. This allows for a much more solid exposure to another Christian tradition and gives plenty of opportunities to develop meaningful friendships. If you are a little shy of the idea, ask a friend or two to join you in the adventure. You will be doing them (and the witness of the church of Christ) a favor.

6
Dialogue

· · · · · · · · · · · ·

In our previous suggestion we talked of the need to de-
velop relationships with Christians from different traditions. If
that is a difficult task, building relationships with those outside
the Family will be all the more difficult.

And yet this is where our witness is supposed to send us. Too
often we feel threatened by people who do not know Jesus.
Perhaps we view them as the "enemy." Perhaps we have forgot-
ten that we are not much different from them, with our fears,
aspirations and loves. We need to learn how to listen to people
of other faiths and to people who claim no religious orientation.
We must learn to accept, with respect, that their life's journey
has led them down certain roads of belief, and that their values
and worldviews are as important to them as ours are to us.

Dialogue is an honest, humble exchange of ideas that helps

both parties listen to each other and share their own views with each other. The primary goal is not "conversion" of the other person. It's learning and building a bridge of understanding between two human beings. Dialogue runs contrary to much of our Christian training. We are usually taught what other people believe not by those "other" people, but by someone of our own club. And this teaching usually happens in the context of our being convinced of the evil of the other view.

This process is not entirely honest. And it does not help us develop relationships with people. It trains us to shout our positions at them. It trains us to close our ears to them because we think we already know what they believe.

If you believe God has called you to a future that will take you to people outside the faith (and possibly to other countries), now is the time to begin to learn the art of good dialogue. This is how we suggest you might go about it:

Ask some friends to join you in the process. Make your learning a matter for prayer, asking God for a keen sense of discernment and a humble spirit. Your small group can attend events sponsored by groups with a publicly defined position different from yours. Perhaps these will include a secular organization on campus that is espousing a certain philosophical view that leaves you uncomfortable, or a religious group that is considered theologically off the orthodoxy chart (sometimes called "cult"). Listen to the speeches, debates and development of their positions. As the process allows, ask lots of questions.

When it seems sensitive to do so, identify yourself as a Christian who is trying to understand other people's beliefs. You are asking for help to gain a picture from their viewpoint and to compare it with the one you acquired from your own religious group. You may discover that your openness will create an opportunity for warm exchange and long-term friendship.

This process will help you clarify some of your own beliefs and no doubt make you stronger in the faith. You will be challenged at some points, however, to acknowledge the truth of certain views they hold and incorporate those into your worldview. This can be threatening. But we know that all truth is God's truth. And because the church is called to walk in the light, we must be honest in all our exchanges and accept truth no matter what the source. In fact, this kind of honesty builds a bridge for exchange to go both ways. You will find opportunity to make a clear presentation of your commitment to Christ.

You will also discover your need to go deeper in the Word. A family in Los Angeles was approached by Mormons in a door-to-door campaign. Rather than shutting the door because "we are Christians," they agreed to have dialogue over several weeks. Each week's theological discussion would end with refreshments and friendly chitchat, and as soon as the Mormons were out the door, the family was on the phone to friends with requests for help. Issues were being raised that required deeper plunges into the Scripture. Not a bad outcome for dialogue.

Be sure to continue in prayer throughout this whole process of dialogue. As a group, pray for the people you have been meeting. Ask God to deepen your love for them and to help you be genuine listeners. This approach will prevent you from raising barriers between yourselves and people of other faiths. The opposite outcome is what you're after: letting down the drawbridge to allow people into *your* world.

7
Host Internationals

· · · · · · · · · · ·

The United States is virtual flypaper to people of other
nations. To many, it seems to be a land of promise and opportunity for a bright economic future and a place for freedom from
religious or political persecution. We are no longer surprised by
the need to use gestures as well as words in order to communicate with a stranger on the streets. All the world's fashions and
foods can be bought here. And the city of Los Angeles is now
referred to as the capital of the Third World.

We are fortunate to have this influx of people from around the
world. There are three distinct advantages. First, we are given

the pleasure of meeting new members of God's creation. The handiwork of the Great Artist is showing up on our doorsteps. We can enjoy and learn from the cultures of these people—and thank God for how they enrich our lives.

Second, the presence of these people is a constant reminder to us that the family of God is as wide as the world. We can develop friendships with brothers and sisters in Christ whose names and hometowns are almost impossible for us to pronounce at first. (Make the effort, though! It will mean a lot to them.) Christian immigrants are living evidence to us that God's mercy knows no boundaries. We have the opportunity to lean on them as part of the body of Christ, as well as to offer them help.

And third, the influx of people from around the world is providing us the opportunity to share our love for Christ with people who may not know him. It is as though we were in the marketplace on the day of Pentecost. Everywhere we turn, people speak a different language, claim a different lord.

Here is how you might want to move forward on some of these ideas:

☐ Look up churches that have foreign titles. See if you can meet with the pastor or other staff. Explain your interest in getting to know Christians from other countries and ask what would be the most appropriate way to participate in their fellowship.

☐ Contact your local university. Tell them you are interested in hosting international students for dinner. If you are able to plan in advance, some universities will gladly let you meet students upon their arrival to the country. You'll have the fun of introducing them to several aspects of life in this country.

☐ Contact International Students, Incorporated (ISI) for specific ideas on how to serve international students (see their address in our "Resources" section). They are a Christian organization and will offer you wonderful advice on reaching out to friends from abroad.

8

Host Missionaries

There are currently some 40,000 career missionaries
serving abroad. Every couple of years or so they return to the
United States to update the church here on the progress of their
work. Many of us have childhood memories of watching missionaries share their work. Those were the days when missionaries
were gone for seven years at a stretch. The dear souls were
unaware of the changes that had gone on in their home culture
while they were abroad. They were out of touch regarding latest
fashion, ideas, technology and speech. Little did they know that
on Sunday *they* were the real show—not their malfunctioning
slide projector.

But somehow these wonderful people of God got through to us. They had a corner on the kingdom, it seemed. There was something mysterious and wild about these folks. They knew how to pray, they treasured their Bibles and they could stretch a dime to a dollar. Their sincere love for Jesus spoke volumes, and many of us were moved to a deeper commitment to the world because of them.

We think families should take advantage of these roving gold mines. Here's what to do: Ask your pastor if you could be host to missionaries as they come through your area. Plan in advance. Coordinate with your family schedule to be sure the kids get in some quality time too. Here are some of the ways to let visiting missionaries rub off on your family:

☐ Ask them to lead a nightly time of corporate prayer before everyone is tucked into bed. Their prayers will give your family a glimpse into their lives and their faith.

☐ Ask them to lead a special family Bible study during one of their nights with you.

☐ Have a story night where they tell the unbelievable events to their lives "over there." You will have a chance to laugh and be amazed. The work of God will become fresh to you as you hear someone uncover the fresh drama of God alive in the world today.

☐ Ask them to tell their personal histories. How did God work with them in their youth? What major spiritual battles did they face in their younger years of discipleship? How have those lessons carried over to the years on the mission field?

☐ Turn over the kitchen to them for an evening meal. Get ready for some pretty exotic cuisine!

☐ Get personal. Share your own current struggles in the faith. This may be a sovereign encounter designed by God to help you in a dry or difficult stretch of your walk. And, by the way, be sensitive to their personal needs. Sometimes missionaries give out all the time and receive very little back. You might just be God's angel to them in their time of trial.

9

Zero In
on a Country

· · · · · · · · · · ·

BANGLADESH

Dacca•

The world is just too big for us to wrap our arms around.
We easily become discouraged by the overwhelming number of
languages, the variety of needs and the confusing, even conflict-
ing, accounts of what is going on in the political realm. Paral-
ysis sets in and we do nothing.

One mission leader has said that the answer to this dilemma
is to become a generalist as far as the globe is concerned and
a specialist concerning one specific country. Through this one
country, we'll begin to grasp a fresh vision of God's love at an
international level and to see the possibility of making some

sense of today's spinning sphere. We are moved to action when we are able to visualize the world in smaller chunks.

Some people have told us that this approach has been the very means God used to move them into mission service. As they prayed, read and shared the stories of their favorite country, they discovered a growing desire to move there and become an ambassador of God's love. We like the idea. Here are some ways to move with it:

☐ Ask your local librarian for recent books that tell the story of "your" country. Look for the history, politics, religion, literature and customs. Make a goal of reading two or three books a year. If you belong to a regular prayer group, ask if you might give a ten-minute review of the book and let that lead into prayer.

☐ Go to your local library at least once a week. Skim all the newsmagazines to locate any stories on the country of your choice. Read what you find. If there is something of particular interest, photocopy it. Do the same with newspapers.

☐ Get a large wall map of the country and decorate a corner of your house using it plus items from that part of the world— fabric, carved animals, baskets, photos, whatever you have. Begin to memorize the map. Learn the states, counties, provinces, major cities, agricultural products, industry, waterways, wildlife and bordering countries.

☐ Pray over the map. Involve friends in this. Get a copy of *Operation World* to assist you (see "Resources" section).

☐ Try to find local restaurants and stores from that region of the world. Become familiar with the diet, clothing and commerce.

☐ If you are able to meet people from that part of the world, ask them to teach you about their country. This is a warm compliment to a visitor and a great way to get personal tutoring.

☐ Watch for PBS specials on the country.

☐ If you are able, save up to make a special trip to that nation. If you have developed friendships with people from there, ask them to help you set up your itinerary.

10

Go for the Arts

· · · · · · · · · · ·

One of the advantages of living in today's world is that the globe keeps shrinking due to technology. With the help of CNN, the BBC and other media giants, we are able to stay current on the news in any part of the world, including issues as critical as floods and wars and as mundane as the barometer reading.

Getting beyond the basic facts, cultivate the opportunity to learn about the art of other countries and cultures. Art is the language of the soul. That is how God created us, and this is one sure way to link with the soul of another nation. Societies breathe their pain, hopes, passions and beliefs through the medium of art. We think it makes good sense to grow in our love of global art. Here are some of the ways to forge ahead:

☐ Check your paper for local music or art shows that feature international artists.

☐ Read the art column of the *Christian Science Monitor* at your local library. It regularly covers international art.

☐ Peruse the international contemporary music scene at your local music store. Tell the clerk you want to broaden your exposure to international artists. Also check with the music department at your local university or city college. Try to build appreciation for two or three artists and then expand from there.

☐ Read the book review section of the *New York Times* for international material. Ask your librarian and local university professor to recommend a few good novelists and poets who are currently being published and whose works would make good jumping-off points.

☐ Collect a few articles of clothing that reflect the artistic flair of a national group.

☐ Watch for PBS specials on the art world.

☐ Listen to the soundtracks of movies that are international.

☐ If you are able to befriend internationals, ask them to guide you through the various art forms of their country. If you are ambitious enough, this could become a once-a-month affair that you organize for several friends from your church or fellowship.

11

Find a Mentor

· · · · · · · · · · ·

One of the great treasures of the Christian Family is
people—people who over the years have lived exceptional lives
of love, faith, courage and vision. We have all bumped into
them, either in person or through their writings. We admire
their willingness to stand in the gap, their tenacious grip on
values that transcend the pitiful patterns of our culture and even
our church. We find ourselves thirsting for the key to their
happiness and satisfaction.

The reason we admire them is that we know how difficult it
is to live for the kingdom. Being committed to God's call to

bring justice and mercy to the earth is no easy road. We are so quickly ensnared by the cares of making a living and pursuing our own comfort. Great dreams and resolutions dissolve all too soon into wishful notes in a journal.

We believe in the goodness of God's character. We believe that the desire in our hearts to do good to others is from God, who wills good for all his creation. And God does not intend to frustrate our ambition to live compassionate lives. He will equip us with whatever is required to fulfill the passion he has placed in our hearts. But we need to understand that God did not create "Lone Ranger" activists. He gave us special gifts that can be a salve to the hurting world, but he also created us with the need to be linked to others as we put our gifts into action. We cannot expect to live fruitful lives of ministry if we intend to "go it alone."

One of our suggestions, then, is to link up with a mentor.

Is there someone whose ministry to the world is an inspiration to you? Someone who not only talks grand words but lives a grand life of service to others? Someone who manages to filter out the pull of society's agenda and connect instead with the blind, crippled, lost, oppressed and hungry? If so, attach yourself to that saint and learn all you can! Here are a few ways you can do that:

☐ Collect the person's writings and ask a friend or two to join you for a special study of those materials.

☐ If the person is currently engaged in a local ministry, seek ways to volunteer your time and observe how he or she lives in the middle of the pain.

☐ Write a letter expressing your interest to find a mentor. Share your familiarity with this person's ministry and tell some of the ways you have been impacted in your walk with Christ and desire to live in the world's pain. Ask if there is some way you could brush against his or her life, be it in correspondence or an occasional visit.

☐ If the person is also a public speaker, perhaps you could arrange a workshop that features an address by the person and open discussion time. Arrange ahead of time to build in personal interaction. If the idea works, you could repeat it annually.

☐ You may have the luxury of living near a mentor who is interested in contributing regularly to your life—perhaps through weekly sessions of prayer and Bible study. Embrace those opportunities! They do not come easily, and they are a privilege.

12
Question Your Categories
· · · · · · · · · · · ·

Being committed to the world mission of the church
requires bumping against people who are quite different from
ourselves. In a previous chapter we encouraged the idea of getting outside our comfort zones and allowing new experiences
and people to stretch our world. We want to expand on that idea
a little.

We are not always aware of the prejudices we carry against
others. They have many forms of expression: calling Arabs people who bury their heads in the sand, referring to frugal people
as Scotch, using the phrase "jewing down," calling homosexu-

als faggots, talking about women as girls, labeling blondes dumb or Mexicans lazy. We employ this language more than we know. We need to understand that it is offensive to the people who bear the brunt of our laughter. And we need to understand that this offensive behavior works in direct opposition to the worldwide ministry of the kingdom, which breaks down the barriers that divide, gives honor to the weak, invites all to the banquet table of God's mercy, esteems others more highly than ourselves.

The book of Revelation offers a picture of all the nations gathered together around the feet of the Lord. Every one of them will be represented at the final hour when his mercy encompasses every tribe, tongue and nation. We need to exercise the discipline of asking ourselves about our own racism, prejudice and sexism. The blood of Christ was shed for all people! We do not have the right by our parochial attitudes to label others as less deserving of God's mercy. And we certainly do not have the right to elevate ourselves above the rest of God's special creation. Here are a few suggestions for dealing with the prejudices that so naturally develop among us.

First, understand that you are making a commitment to take a public risk. Most racism or sexism is expressed in the open. You are making a decision to put away the malicious tongue, to stand for the beauty of God's handiwork. It is not easy to go down this road, because you encounter the anger of others who would prefer that you just let the prejudices remain. Understand that all too often we feel better about ourselves when we tear others down. (This is an indication of a poor self-image and says volumes about our need to accept ourselves as God's precious creation.)

☐ Be quick to apologize to another when you make a racist or sexist comment.

☐ Ask people who are the object of this kind of ridicule how it makes them feel. Explain your desire to grow beyond those natural patterns; ask them for ideas on how to do it.

☐ Cultivate an interest in their contributions to society. For example, much of the "Spanish" architecture of the West was designed by Muslims. Learn of these contributions and give credit where it is due.

☐ Be quick to hear their preferences. People used to mock African-Americans who said they disliked the word *nigger*. They felt the same about changing vocabulary from *colored* to *black*. Why should we oppose the desire of a people to find words that more comfortably fit their ethnic heritage? We should embrace these requests.

☐ Actively pursue literature, PBS specials and movies that help to sensitize you to the history, contributions and needs of people we commonly marginalize with our unkind language.

☐ Research the history of Native Americans in North America. Make a point of understanding their view of the past, and work hard at adjusting your language and opinions to fit this more accurate understanding.

Those who are labeled unkindly by society should always feel a warm welcome from and companionship with Christians who celebrate all of God's creation. Society should indeed label us as people who are friends to everyone—red, brown, yellow, black and white.

13

Diet of
Words

· · · · · · · · · · · ·

We are fortunate to live in a day of information. We
have the pleasure of learning about other people's way of life,
their customs, daily events and hardships. This is a gift of God
to us. Christians naturally want to know about others. God has
built this curiosity into our internal structure and we are blessed
to have the benefit of technology to help us.

This does not mean we are going to naturally embrace a good
diet of words. It's so easy to slip into a diet of junk food, even
though our bodies crave healthy nutrition. And so it is with the
diet of the mind. We need to make a commitment to a good

routine of *reading,* taking in a healthy selection of materials to enhance our picture of the world. It's as though we have to ensure we are taking in a good balance of each of the food groups.

We suggest you link up with a couple of friends who want to make the same commitment to healthy reading. It is always easier to accomplish in the company of others. Here are a few suggestions for mental food:

☐ Go the library on a regular basis and read several daily papers. A few excellent ones are the *New York Times, Los Angeles Times* and *Christian Science Monitor.* Regular newsmagazines include *Time, Newsweek* and *U.S. News and World Report.*

☐ Try to read international newsmagazines that cover the same events. You might be surprised to see how differently they view life. A couple of examples are *South, The Economist* and *World Press Review.*

☐ Read mission publications. We have listed a large selection of magazines, newsletters, journals, annuals and reference books in our "Resources" section.

☐ Take in the missionary classics. Stories of Jim Elliot, William Carey, Lottie Moon and George Mueller always make for inspiring reading. Contemporary stories bound to become classics are *Bruchko* by Bruce Olson, *We Signed Away Our Lives* by Kari Malcolm and *Peace Child* by Don Richardson.

14

Take a Professional Detour

· · · · · · · · · · ·

Thousands of companies are ready to provide you with an all-expenses-paid trip abroad. What's the catch? You have to be a little creative and daring.

Professional help is needed at all levels of commerce and government in other countries: accountants, medical workers, bankers, hotel managers, construction engineers, teachers, scientists, agronomists, sanitation specialists, communications experts. If you are willing to add a little spice and adventure to your life, we recommend that you join the pool of U.S. Christians who are on assignment abroad. There are more than 400,000 of them.

The time commitment will range from a few months to a couple years. As for location, there is hardly a spot on the globe that is not open to this kind of creative partnership. The benefits are immediately obvious. You gain the opportunity to grow in your awareness of another nation. You may be considering missionary service to that part of the globe; taking a professional detour becomes a means to "test" yourself and the location.

In addition, these professional detours are an excellent means to relocate where Christians cannot enter on a regular missionary visa. You enter instead as a professional, making a valuable contribution to that society's economic/educational system. Your presence is an honest partnership. And because you are a child of the King, you bring that identity to all your new relationships. And then, of course, all your costs are covered. You will often link up with a group that pays your regular salary, travel costs and the cost of an annual vacation back home. Each placement differs in relation to family requirements. If you are highly skilled in a narrow market, you can often "write your own ticket."

If you don't know where to start, contact Global Outreach. This is a Christian placement company and can get you started. They carry a database of current openings around the world and can tell you of jobs that match your skill and need. They are listed in the "Resources" section.

If you would like to take a shot at teaching English in Asia, contact Educational Services, Inc. (ESI) or English Language Institute in China (ELIC). Both of these groups have a good track record of placing people in summer, one-year and two-year assignments.

You may also find help in your professional association. Newsletters will often billboard foreign placement options and give you directions on how to pursue these opportunities. If you are studying at a university, make an appointment with the career counselor. The career office often carries long lists of crosscultural assignments that do not pay top dollar but do cover your costs adequately plus pay a small salary. These are good beginning points if you want to make a career of detouring!

If you already have extensive experience abroad, contact Christian relief and development organizations. They regularly need someone who can jump into a temporary assignment without having to go through all the crosscultural orientation.

15
Study Abroad

· · · · · · · · · · · ·

If you are on an educational track that is going to con-
sume the next several years of your life, we'd like to recommend
that you build some foreign study into your academic program.
The cost of living abroad is usually assumed in the academic
package, and so you avoid the room-and-board expenses you
would incur if you were taking a regular vacation in the same
country.

There are other good reasons to opt for this academic approach:

☐ If you want to grow in your understanding of God's heart for the world, this is a very cost-effective way to get your feet wet.

☐ If you are not sure you can find your way around another country, doing it as part of an academic program gives you the advantage of having a host whose goal is to give you a first-class experience during your stay. And you see the country from the viewpoint of a national rather than a tourist agency—always a plus.

☐ Overseas academic credit looks good on a transcript later, when you are looking for employment. Your potential supervisor will read this as an indication that you are innovative, motivated and growing.

☐ More specifically, if you are interested in working abroad, your transcript will show a steady, long-term interest in that direction. Employers like to know that your idea of accepting foreign placement isn't some sudden whim that came with the previous night's hot sauce.

If you are studying at a secular university, meet with your academic adviser to see what options you have in your field of study. If you are studying at a Christian college, those same options are available to you. But you also have the added benefit of the international Christian network. Talk to visiting missionaries about international Bible colleges. Several mission organizations are in partnership with Bible schools that have two- to four-year academic programs. You could very well study at one of these institutions for a year (in Singapore or South Africa, for example) and pay less for a full year's tuition, room, board and travel than you would for one semester in the United States. These credits can be transferred into your regular academic program back at the Christian college from which you plan to graduate.

Not only will you add a good selling point to your transcript, you will also grow in your understanding of the world, gain international friends and open the door to service opportunities abroad.

16

Vacation with a Purpose

· · · · · · · · · · · ·

We stole this title because we really like it. This idea is the brainchild of two enterprising Christians in their thirties. The idea has taken off like fire to a dry field! And so they have put their concept into a handy book and leader's guide entitled *Vacations with a Purpose: A Planning Handbook for Your Short-Term Missions Team.* See our "Resources" section for ordering information.

Most of us love to take vacations. One of the caricatures of our country is the motor home with BBQ and TV antenna to boot. Not that everyone does it that way, but we do love a good time away from the hustle and bustle of work and daily home routines. The idea of Vacations with a Purpose (VWAP) is to create a happy medium between the jungle-slogging, mosquito-infested mission trip and the leave-me-alone-with-my-TV vacation that shuts out the rest of the world. And these vacations with a purpose are not meant to stick us out in the unknown by ourselves. The idea is to go with a team of people who are ready to have fun together in a new environment. The team also links up with Christians in another culture who become partners in this adventure to the world. Because the concept is to build this into your regular vacation routine, the authors of VWAP suggest you choose a location that is close to home—at least in the same hemisphere. That way you aren't facing a budget buster.

We hope you will give it a shot. The book is packed with very helpful information to help you plan all the details from getting vaccinations to keeping a file of emergency information. We have also listed a resource organization, BridgeBuilders, which can help if you want special assistance in planning your trip.

A variation on this theme is to pick a domestic location that may be just a few hours away. This is much more workable for many folks because of financial and time constraints. There are several ministries working in the inner cities or just across the border which host Christians who want to learn more about ministry. We have listed some of those organizations in the back too. You will see there are both urban and rural options.

17
Create an Internship

. . . .

Most seminary and graduate school programs today
require some kind of internship that helps you get practical with
your knowledge. These internships can range from a few hours
to a full year.

Our suggestion is that you simply attach your interest in the
world to these internship requirements. Let your professor or
academic adviser know of your desire to become involved cross-
culturally. Ask for a placement that will take you outside your
comfort zone. For example, if your program requires that you
spend several hours each week volunteering at a church, ask to

be assigned to a church of a different ethnicity than your own. If you are in an economic program, ask to be assigned to an urban ministry that is seeking innovative means to empower the poor. We have suggested some groups in the "Resources" section.

If you are studying at a secular institution, you will need to carefully prepare the case for the internship of your choice. These institutions want to be sure your placement is not just a watered-down religious experience but a solid, practical application of the classroom material. This is a reasonable requirement, so work with your adviser.

Your course of study may not require you to have an internship. Don't let that deter you! Meet with your adviser and communicate your desire to build an internship into your academic program. You will probably be able to design a program that satisfies some of the typical graduation prerequisites.

Some students find that the financial demands of school prohibit an unpaid internship. All the extra hours are consumed with part-time jobs to pay the cost of learning. Again, this may be the time for innovation. Many denominations and local churches will "support" you during your internship. They'll pay you a regular monthly stipend in relation to the number of hours you put into the church or parachurch work. Be sure to ask around to see whether this option is open to you. Denominational structures understand the value of having graduates come to them with more than just a classroom degree under their belt.

18
Get Credit for Your Summer

· · · · · · · · · · · ·

If you are in college, this idea is for you.

Many students want to travel abroad to explore the art of the Louvre, the battle places of Napoleon, the heights of the Himalayas or the wonders of the rain forests. All of these interests (and many more) have very natural connections to academic requirements. The key is to make that connection for your academic adviser. It always makes sense to let life's experiences do "double duty" when possible. Learning does not always translate to academic credit, but sometimes you can arrange for it to do so!

Here is what you do. Think through how your academic interests fit your travel interests. For example, you are studying environmental science. Messiah College has an expert on the subject—Professor Joe Sheldon. More than that, you have learned that Professor Sheldon has conducted summer crosscultural trips up the Amazon. Step one is to get all the information on the program. You need to communicate your interest in doing this as part of your degree program at your own school. Make sure you will be able to be a part of a scheduled trip if your adviser agrees to it.

Step two is to look through your school catalog to establish whether such a trip fits into the general requirements of academic internships or special study options. Step three is to type up a proposal for your academic adviser. Be sure to think through all the details that will be important to this person: credentials of the professor leading the course, amount of reading, amount of lecture time, any paper or exam requirements, total actual hours in the program. Present your proposal as an initial draft for discussion purposes. This allows you the freedom to adjust it to fit the adviser's requirements.

Some students have been able to make a clear connection between their major in mission or religious studies and an overseas experience, such as a summer in India working with national Christians in a church-planting program. If you are unable to find a program that you think will work, be innovative enough to design one with the help of mission leaders, pastors and academic advisers. Thousands of students have done it. They are better prepared to serve after such a learning experience. And, last but not least, some students have been able to justify this kind of travel to parents who are paying the bill. The academic overlay lends credibility to the travel plans.

The idea is valuable, so be sure to work it from every possible angle until you succeed!

19
Prayer

· · · · · · · · · · · ·

Matthew 9 records Jesus' steps through crowds of needy humanity. He is overwhelmed by the sight—so he tells his disciples to form a nonprofit organization to do something about the need.

No, of course he doesn't. Neither does he tell them to call together religious leaders to form an action committee, nor does he tell his followers to get on the next missionary ship. Rather, he instructs his disciples to *pray.* "Ask the Lord of the harvest, therefore, to send out workers into his harvest field" (Mt 9:38).

We believe that prayer is as basic as ministry gets. It is possible to be a high-powered activist who on the outside seems to overturn the world for Christ but who all the while is inactive and lazy in the inner person—undisciplined in the art of sitting at the feet of Jesus, groaning the prayers of one touched by the pain that disturbs our Lord. Activism is no substitute for prayer. In fact, activism has to grow out of prayer.

This should be good news to us, really, because it underlines the truth that *this is God's world*. For us, ministry is a privilege, a cooperative effort with Christ. We do not fret and worry about the harvest. Rather, in the quiet of our sanctuary we acquire the heart of God for that harvest, and then we move as we sense the hand of the Lord nudging us. One day we will stand amazed in heaven as we witness God's warm reception for all the unknown warriors who did their hard work in the prayer closet.

If you want to develop the ministry of prayer, there are resources to help you. We have a few suggestions:

☐ Contact Concerts of Prayer, International. This ministry has its roots solidly in a tradition of world mission. The organization has several books that will help you develop an understanding of the role of prayer. And it offers a package of materials that will help you sponsor your own citywide prayer rally. Prayer takes on the dual focus of lifting up our own nation's ills and those of the world. Thousands of Christians are getting together in these concerts of prayer—you will be joining a good thing.

☐ Get a copy of *Operation World*. It will take you through each country of the world, one by one, over the course of a year. Information includes the spread of the gospel, economic conditions and the state of the national church.

☐ Buy a copy of the Prayer Diary from Youth With A Mission. It does double duty as a management tool and a prayer prompter. For each day, right beside the space for you to list your daily appointments and assignments, there are snippets of information that become good prayer items and space to record the special prayer concerns you bring regularly to the Lord.

Prayer is vital. That is probably why it is so difficult to have a healthy prayer life—we are at odds with the kingdom of darkness. If you have tried before but always come away discouraged, recruit a friend who will help you slowly build up the discipline of prayer until you begin to reap the rewards of going to the sanctuary alone.

20
Time

· · · · · · · · · · · ·

In the other four 50 Ways books, as we wrote about ways to make a difference in the world, we found that time is a thread common to all of them. (As we asked people for their advice on what to put in these guides, all of them assured us that time would be a chief barrier to becoming involved.)

We have written this and the other four guides to help you put your desires into motion. These books are not intended to clobber readers with all the kinds of things they "ought to be doing." Rather, they offer a variety of options that may fit into your life as ways to make a difference for the kingdom. So, as we look at the issue of time, we are not interested in saying, "Get out there—put more time into kingdom work!" We are saying, "Organize your time so that the things you sincerely want to do for the kingdom will happen."

Actually, time is our friend. It is a gift from God. We have the freedom to arrange it in a way that reflects our sense of call and our sensibilities for health. But it is like any of life's other gifts: we have to learn how best to work with it. There are ups and downs, the sense of failure, the feeling of just the right fit. Our advice is: Be patient, experiment, take charge of your life and enjoy the process.

Quite a mouthful.

Begin by deciding how many hours each month you would like to give to the needs of the world. Ask a friend who knows you to help you figure this one out. You may even want to depersonalize this a little and decide how many hours the two of you will spend together doing something for the kingdom. Once you have locked in on a number, page through this book and choose a few items that would fit that time commitment. Experiment. See how it goes for a couple of weeks and then adjust.

And think of the year as a whole. Do you want to give a week, in addition, to a special trip abroad or in a local urban community? Is there some kind of academic/vocational goal you have for the year in relation to your desire to make a difference in the world? Build that into your time.

We are told to "redeem" the time because the days are evil. That is not a burdensome, guilt-laden requirement, meant to leave us feeling rotten when we sit back to listen to our favorite music. It is a call to let our time work in favor of God's agenda instead of just slipping away. A call to let time blossom with the fruit of wholeness and health, compassion and resolve.

21
Money and Mission

· · · · · · · · · · · ·

The success of the mission enterprise depends on
Christians who are willing to separate from their hard-earned
money. It is appropriate that even the means for supporting
world outreach is selfless giving. We do not receive a service or
product in return for the money. Our "customer satisfaction,"
if you will, is the pleasure of cooperating with Christ in spread-
ing abroad the far-reaching love of Calvary.

We think it is important to resist giving under duress. There
are many reasons for this. The Scripture tells us that God loves
a cheerful giver. Funds given "under obligation" are not joyful

dollars. We must accept the fact that God does not *need* our money. Our giving is a kind of fellowship with Christ, one that we enter voluntarily and with anticipation.

When we give out of a sense of dogged obedience we feel we have done our "duty." Our giving is reduced to a contractual activity: Christ died for me so I have to give to mission work. We may not say it this clearly, but that attitude lurks.

And when we give under the pressure of a good sales job (emotional appeals, emergency, "if-you-don't-who-will") we eventually tire of giving because we realize there are just too many emergencies to match our dollars. We may even eventually resent the people who so craftily separated us from our funds.

Our advice is to give out of a genuine sense that you have connected with a person or ministry reflecting your own heart's commitments. To give to them is to extend the reach of your own values and God-given desires. Some would protest this approach—perhaps because it does not sound drastic enough. "Not enough sacrifice in there," we might hear. Our response is simply that we do not believe sacrifice is a public affair. "Do not let your left hand know what your right hand is doing," Jesus said (Mt 6:3). We cannot presume to judge "good giving" by how much flows from someone's pocket into the coffers. Jesus shocked the disciples with his assertion that the widow who gave a mere mite was giving more to the work of the kingdom than the Pharisees who poured their gold coins into the temple boxes. God looks on the heart and from his viewpoint he saw what they could not (and what *we* cannot).

We face two temptations with our giving—the desire to win the approval of God and others and the desire to "settle accounts" with God. We must resist both. And those who are in positions of leadership, who regularly make appeals for funds, must resist the temptation of playing into these weaknesses.

Giving is a joyful affair. We recommend that you listen to God for ways to give money to ministries that are already a part of your life. It is good to give where there is already a relationship in place. We also recommend that you experience the fun of giving to a variety of mission causes. It is a blessing to know that your money has been able to advance the work of God on several fronts. Look for ministries that plant churches where the gospel has never gone, organizations that work to relieve the stress of the oppressed, ministries that feed the hungry and groups that work to care for the earth. All of these fall under the canopy of God's character, which means they are also embedded in our character.

Beware, though, of taking on so many causes that your interest and prayers become scattered. Better to give and pray regularly for a certain few to whom you'll be faithful over a number of years. And if you give on a rotating basis (a larger check to A this month, B next month and C the next, rather than a small check each month to each of them), you'll save each group some receipting costs.

A final suggestion for giving has to do with non-Western organizations. There is a growing movement to look for ways to become partners with Third World Christian efforts. Nationals are usually much better equipped than foreign missionaries to do the job of outreach at a local level. And they usually are able to do it for much less. It is not uncommon to find that the money used to support one Western missionary family could have supported ten national families in the same work. We need to be sensible in our stewardship. Refer to the "Resources" section where we have listed several Third World organizations worthy of our support.

You may wish you had more to give—wish things like birthday presents and wedding gifts didn't demand so much of your cash. For a way to honor your friend's or relative's special day while supporting self-development projects among poor people who need a way to earn a living, write for an Alternative Gift Catalog (address in the back of the book).

Section
2

Your Church
or Fellowship
· · · · · · · · · · · · · · · · ·

22
Organize a Summer Trip

· · · · · · · · · · ·

College groups and churches alike have discovered the power of crosscultural trips. A campus worker told us, "The students always return to campus with a real fire to know more of Christ. I have to work super hard to stay ahead of them!" An urban pastor echoes the observation: "There is no more need to beg for volunteers to work in the nursery or teach Sunday school. It's as though sleepwalkers became conscious."

Campus organizations such as InterVarsity Christian Fellowship, Navigators and Campus Crusade have benefited so much from this phenomenon that they intentionally design these trips as a mechanism for discipleship. And they are joined by thousands of churches that have discovered the same treasure. As many as 250,000 North American Christians venture on a cross-cultural trip each year.

We are enthusiastic about this trend. We want to emphasize that we perceive discipleship to be the primary value of these trips. We are not so excited about the idea of going to another culture to "convert it to Christ" overnight. And there are not too many groups who carry that silly goal any more.

Here are some of the ways churches and fellowships have organized their short-term trips:

☐ An "Easter Week Plunge" into the inner city or across the border to work with staff who have a long-time presence there. These become annual excursions, and over time solid relationships develop which help cement a global commitment.

☐ A summer trip to Russia or China to teach English where the demand is exceptionally high. One campus organization has such a successful track record of this in Russia that they now have the opportunity to develop a values-based curriculum (with full freedom to include the Bible) for the entire educational system in one university.

☐ A reconciliation trip to a strife-torn area in South Africa or the Middle East. Students and church members put together ethnically diverse teams to cooperate with national Christians who are trying to establish an alternative to the bitter separations that have developed over the decades.

☐ A six-month research trip to an ethnic group that has very little contact with Christians. These teams return home with hearts (and slides) that will help call others into a concerted work of church planting in that region.

☐ A ten-day trip to a mission station to help in the construction of a dormitory for missionary kids. Church members are able to contribute their manual labor skills and gain exposure to another culture at the same time. All during the vacation days.

Fortunately, there are several groups waiting to serve churches and fellowships that want to design crosscultural trips. We have listed those under "Service Organizations" in the "Resources" section. There are short-term mission organizations whose exclusive focus is designing quality crosscultural trips. We have listed several of these. Be sure to check out career mission agencies too. They understand the value of offering quality short-term mission experiences. The current group of North American missionaries identifies a short-term mission trip as the chief means God used to "recruit" many of them for missionary service. And don't overlook your own denomination. Several have created national short-term programs that will offer you rural, urban and international team experiences of various lengths.

23

Organize an Action Committee

· · · · · · · · · · ·

In the 1970s an innovative group of church and mission leaders got together to form the Association of Church Mission Committees—now called simply ACMC. Their goal was to think of every possible way to encourage the local church to embrace the vision of discipling the nations. Their primary means would be to work through local church committees that had the same goal. The effort has been a screaming success. It is perhaps the single most important "quiet revolution" at the local church level as far as mission from North America is concerned. In the late 1980s a parallel group, the Association of

International Mission Services (AIMS), was formed. It took on a similar goal but focused its energies on the independent charismatic churches. The organization is trying to keep up with the eager demands for its services.

Our suggestion follows on the function of these two groups. We suggest that your local church or fellowship form an action group whose goal is to think through ways to keep the mission vision fresh. This same group can become the locus for hosting missionaries, raising support, assembling short-term mission teams and helping the church respond to unique global needs.

Call a meeting of people who would like to volunteer their time for such an action committee. Pray together that the Lord will unite you around the vision of his kingdom. Pray for the variety of needs in the world—from the lost to the hungry to the oppressed. Ask God to give you the wisdom and skill necessary to hold a vision of the world in front of church members and win their support. Here are some of the initial ways to kick off your efforts:

☐ Host a special "global briefing" banquet for people in the church who would like to explore the world. Entertain them with good food and music. Have an animated speaker talk about the world today and end with an application for local involvement. Ask people to fill out a simple questionnaire on what skills and interests they have and what kinds of things the committee could do to serve them. Put together a simple first-year game plan based on their input. Make the goals easily achievable and work hard to "scratch people where they itch." If you want to have a successful second year, people must be impressed with the first round.

☐ Involve the pastor and other key church staff in your mission vision. Several churches organize annual trips for their pastors. The pastors usually take a few elders along and stop over in three or four countries with the object of learning about ways God is at work. They can often serve the missionaries by speaking to groups and offering encouragement to individuals along the way. These motivating trips keep the world in front of the pastor (and the church) all year long.

☐ Invite people to bring special local needs to the committee. Together you can brainstorm ways to respond to the needs. A good idea can be taken to the congregation or fellowship group for corporate support. Over time this committee becomes the lightning rod for needs as well as the engine that drives an outward-looking vision.

24
Adopt-A-People

There are as many as a billion people who are mem-bers of ethnic groups that have no indigenous church. That means their understanding of the gospel is that it is a foreign religion. It does not speak their own tongue or have their own people leading the way. These groups are popularly known as the Unreached Peoples.

We suggest that your church "adopt" one of these groups. There is plenty of help if this is a goal that interests you. You'll find the Adopt-A-People address in our "Resources" section. Here are some of the ways to implement the program:

☐ Pray as a team for a sense of God's guidance about which group you should adopt. If there are people in your church or fellowship who are ethnically close to one of these people groups, that could provide a natural bridge to help you in your goal.

☐ Put together a profile of these people for your fellowship. Perhaps you could create an attractive brochure with the voluntary help of an artist who is committed to the program. Include this handout as part of the church bulletins on a certain Sunday (ask for the chance to explain it in a "Mission Minute" during the service) and keep a supply on hand for newcomers.

☐ Create an attractive display about this group, on a table or bulletin board at church. Raid magazines and books for good photos and write-ups. Be sure to include a map in your display to give a good reference point.

☐ Each Sunday, have a minute of prayer for this group. Share clippings from the week's newspaper that have some impact, direct or indirect, on your adopted people group.

☐ Put together a research team to go and visit this group. You may be able to pull in the expertise of a mission agency to help you in this phase. Videotape your excursion and share the results with the entire church.

☐ Look for ways in which fellowship members can take professional detours to that ethnic group (see idea 14 in this book).

☐ Talk with mission agency leaders and the Adopt-A-People organization for help to engage in a formal church planting effort to that group. If you discover that others have also directed their energies to this particular group, praise the Lord. Put competition aside and see if you can join your energies with them.

☐ Encourage fellowship members to pray about the possibility of going to that group as career missionaries. It's a massive commitment. Decide ahead of time to support your own, so that this becomes an effort of the entire congregation.

☐ Organize regular short-term mission trips to this people group so that many members of your fellowship begin to feel personally attached to the vision.

25
Adopt-A-Country

The political lines are constantly being redrawn in our modern world. Just when we are sure we have all the flags memorized, another nation divides into three smaller ones!

We think it would be both educational and fun to "adopt" a different country each year. The goal would be for the fellowship to build a deepening awareness of the nations of the world as well as a sense of how Christians can be involved in helping with kingdom work in those different nations. Here are some ways to implement this idea:

☐ Organize a team to take responsibility for this project. As with our other ideas, we encourage you to build a very strong base through group prayer. Ask God to make this *his* project; pray for wisdom to implement the ideas in ways that are genuinely helpful to members of the fellowship.

☐ Locate a place in the church or fellowship room that can become a growing theater of the nations. Each year you will add another country to this display. It could include photo books, maps, clippings from magazines and current newspapers, the flag, cookbooks from that region, art, clothes, musical instruments, charts showing economic, religious and political details.

☐ Begin with small, "exotic" countries. Involve people's imaginations. Make the process fun and engaging. The idea is to build a desire to learn more about the world and seek ways to become personally involved.

☐ Every Sunday, have a small item in the bulletin that gives that week's latest news, and add interesting tidbits. Think of it—everyone in your group will be getting fifty-two "mini" geography lessons on one country.

☐ Look for opportunities to bring people from that country to your group. This does not require any big expense—if you look hard enough they probably live within a few miles of you.

☐ Take advantage of local events that feature your adopted country. These may be in the form of music, drama, cuisine or even a political rally.

☐ Perhaps you could top off the year by asking the Lord to help you use Christmas as an occasion for responding to this country that has now become so familiar to you. Ask nationals and mission organizations for ideas on specific needs which a special love offering (of cash or other gifts, as appropriate) might meet and suggestions for where to send it.

26
Twin Up

A growing number of churches have been looking for ways to be more closely linked to other churches around the world. This desire grows out of several concerns. First, they are no longer satisfied to send money blindly. This isn't an accountability issue—it's relational. These churches want to know that there are real people at the other end of their gift check. Second, they are bothered by a sense that the relationship is paternalistic: we give to those poor folks because they really need our help. Such one-sidedness does not make for a healthy long-term relationship. Third, they realize that we Western churches need some of the wealth of non-Western churches. They demonstrate a quality of spirituality which we desire for ourselves and our own fellowships. We need to receive from them.

So the equation is changed to "twinning." We are twins, partners, each giving to the other, each receiving from the other. In some ways this is parallel to the idea of sister cities.

We think this is a healthy development in mission. It's more in line with the idea that we are all members of the same body— each in need of the contribution the other part makes to the whole. If your group wants to twin with another church, one approach is to contact the group called Harvest (listed in the "Resources" section). They specialize in linking churches to each other. Here are some additional advantages of twinning:

☐ A steady long-term base develops across the border that makes short-term trips much easier to organize.

☐ You are able to have members from that church come for a short-term visit to your community. The ramifications are wonderful.

☐ Crosscultural internships are easily arranged for college students who attend your congregation.

☐ Your church becomes free of the old, paternalistic approach to mission. Instead, it now celebrates the life of a truly global church that has linked its arms across the ocean to disciple the nations as full partners.

☐ Being linked to that church has a way of keeping issues in your own culture in focus. Materialism, the broken family and stress caused by the rat race take on new dimensions. You actually become better equipped to see your own society for what it is and you find yourself more effective as a Christian at home. Meanwhile, your personal concern and practical sharing can be a tremendous encouragement to your twin congregation.

27
Mission Sunday

· · · · · · · · · · · ·

Organize a special Sunday once a year that has mis-
sion as its exclusive focus.

There are many ways to make the day a success. We will
recommend several ideas, but first a couple of cautions.

First, people have too often carried forward the concept that
the missionary enterprise is old-fashioned, something for individuals who are out of touch, not quite current in their understanding of society. There is some truth to this, of course. It is
difficult for missionaries to stay current with their "home" culture while they are working hard to understand their host cul-

ture. That's part of the price they pay to work abroad.

Just a couple of decades ago, missionaries were returning home for a sabbatical only once every seven years or so. And communication was nothing like it is today (the video camera, notebook computer, MTV, private satellite dishes, CNN and portable phones are but a few years old). Consequently, missionaries were virtually cut off from their home culture while abroad. Returning home always meant traumatic culture shock in reverse.

But the stereotype of a missionary as "out of touch" is not an accurate reflection of the missionary task—a discipline that involves every bit of our creative minds, every ounce of our energy and every gift of the Holy Spirit. There is no task more demanding and rewarding. Fortunately, some of God's choicest servants have chosen missionary careers.

Our second caution is this: Be careful not to paint mission as something *we* do to people *over there*. This has the potential of stirring up old stereotypes of the Great White Missionary. Include needs both at home and abroad.

Here are some ideas for your mission Sunday:

☐ Bring in a special speaker from some other country to share the biblical basis of mission for the sermon. Be sure to choose someone who can include stories of how his or her own people go as missionaries to distant lands. This helps make us all equal at the foot of the cross and reminds us that not all missionaries are from our own country.

☐ Get some first-class international musicians to do special music that morning. Rely on help from nearby universities if necessary.

☐ Ask a local ministry to give a ten-minute presentation of its work in your city.

☐ If your fellowship has its own homegrown missionaries, have one of them do a ten-minute presentation on his or her work.

☐ Ask each Sunday-school teacher to make the focus of that week's lesson God's call to disciple the nations.

☐ Display literature in the entryway for people who want to explore the subject of mission a little further.

Make sure that the overall tone of the day tantalizes people to want to grow as "world Christians." There is little value in bludgeoning friends with your strong feelings about the globe!

28
Mission Curriculum

· · · · · · · · · · · ·

We mentioned earlier in this book that you may want to link up with some friends to read through the whole Bible while looking for evidences of God's compassionate nature. Now we take the concept a little further.

God's heart for the world is not a tagged-on characteristic—a sort of oh-by-the-way-folks-go-into-all-the-nations benediction. The giving heart of God is the most pervasive theme in all of Scripture. We would go so far as to say it is the very heartbeat of the Bible. It makes sense for Christians to organize ways to become more acquainted with this theme. Here are some curriculum ideas:

☐ Most Sunday-school schedules run on thirteen-week cycles. If you plan to hold a special mission Sunday, consider designing a semester-long follow-up class on God's heart for the world. You can put the content together in any of several ways. Ask a local seminary or Bible college professor or missionary (retired or furloughing) to take on the assignment. If there is no one to fill the slot, see if there are motivated lay activists who would love the challenge of putting together such a course.

☐ Order the Global Issues Bible Study series from IVP. It has twelve study guides, each containing six lessons. You could choose two of them for a semester. Subjects include ministering in the urban world, multiethnicity, healing for broken people, environmental stewardship and so on.

☐ Follow the example of several enterprising Christians we know of: Create a special mission series that is offered on a week-night to Christians from all over your area. This can be a wonderful cooperative event for churches that are interested in pursuing the same idea but want a little company. You could offer a ten-week series on exploring God's heart for the world. People could work through the entire Global Issues Bible Study series. Class members would study one lesson each day in their quiet time; then the group session would be a special presentation on the subject folks had studied all week long.

☐ Use your imagination—design your own content, pull in specialists from the surrounding area, rent videos, study books or analyze the week's news against the biblical call to love the world.

29
Global Festival

· · · · · · · · · · · ·

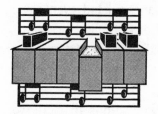

We are used to thinking about the world. International crises come into our homes in living color via TV and newsmagazines, and the ramifications for us as a nation help us realize we are linked to the rest of the human family.

We suggest that your local fellowship or church stage a colorful Global Festival. It makes sense for the church to host this kind of event. Our God created the globe, and the church's shadow reaches every corner of the globe. You could choose to what degree the festival would be evangelistic, overtly Christian or even mission-centered. The event could be a grand missionary celebration involving several local churches, or it could serve as a cultural event that intrinsically reminds Christians of our call to the world and stirs up the curiosity of people outside the church—why are these Christians so current on the international scene?

Here are some components you could include in the festival:

☐ A special musical afternoon where artists are invited to play their ethnic music to the entire group.

☐ A tent for artists to display paintings, sculptures, fabrics and other wares from their own cultures.

☐ Other performance-related events such as poetry readings, dance demonstrations or folk dances.

☐ Booths for local chapters of groups representing other countries (for example, the Chinese-American Organization or the Armenian Center).

☐ Booths for organizations that are working to alleviate the world's suffering. These could be as diverse as Habitat for Humanity, Bread for the World and World Relief.

☐ If you choose to make the focus more closely tied to the church's missionary task, include booths from overseas mission agencies and local ministries that meet people in their pain.

☐ Offer special workshops throughout the day. These could take on a more general theme: apartheid, the new Eastern Europe, AIDS in Africa. They could deal with explicit mission themes if the event is being hosted primarily for Christians.

☐ Have a children's competition for painting and sketching about global themes. Set it up in a tent so that people can watch the process. Give prizes that will stretch the world concern of the children who win, whether a storybook about kids in another country or a share in the sponsorship of an orphan for a year.

☐ Take entries for poems and essays about the world (announce this a month in advance, and repeat the announcement weekly). You might even place a small ad in the paper (if your prizes are attractive enough). Create a panel of judges to select winners.

☐ Ask people to set up snack booths to sell international food. If possible, pay internationals to cook it for you. This will make it authentic, and you probably can find some great cooks. (One Vietnamese church in Chicago is raising funds for a building of its own by selling Vietnamese egg rolls in small and large quantities—*delicious* egg rolls!)

30
Sponsor Seminars

· · · · · · · · · · · ·

Several organizations have already done the hard
work of carefully packaging information on the world. They have
field-tested their material to the point where they now offer a
smooth, interesting and helpful day of focus on a specific need
somewhere in the world. They'll send one or more people to lead
the day for you (costs are very reasonable). All you have to do
is organize the local logistics. Seminar subjects range from
reaching the unreached peoples to feeding the hungry to working for justice to training people who want to sponsor their own
short-term mission trips. We have listed these seminars in the
"Resources" section.

There is not a whole lot more to say about this idea except that we think it makes sense to connect with people who have developed the art of effective communication. And it makes sense to save yourselves some work!

At the logistical level, we would encourage you to involve as many people as possible up front in the planning stages. We know of college students who successfully implemented this idea by creating a special one-time committee to host the event. We have met with pastors who were able to convince five or six other pastors to join in a group effort. Besides pulling a good team together, you will need to secure adequate, inexpensive facilities, provide refreshments and probably offer lunch. You will need to do a first-rate job of promotion and tracking the registrations (that includes handling the money). Someone will need to be in charge of hosting the seminar leaders, making their stay enjoyable.

At the end of the seminar, give people an evaluation sheet asking for their frank evaluation of the event. Include everything from logistics to seminar content. Tell them you are looking for their input to help you decide whether or not to sponsor similar seminars in the future.

31
Budget Priorities

· · · · · · · · · · · ·

Members of a large church in Los Angeles decided to
get serious about their spending priorities. They formed a special
task force to review where the church's money had been spent
over the previous decade. Before the results were released, another committee was formed to put together a priority list—
based on the input of members—for church spending.

The results were not exactly encouraging. The items that were
most important to members were not reflected in the spending
patterns. The church liked to think of itself as globally minded.
And yet the expense summaries showed a church that gave less

than ten percent of its income to international issues and needs.

Members made a forward-thinking decision. They passed a resolution that half of all money taken in by the church would now go automatically to a mission trust fund. A special committee was formed to oversee the disbursements of this fund. There have been some tough choices placed on the church since then. The desires for more pastoral staff, improved facilities and better equipment have often been put on the back burner because the money was not in the general account. And yet the reward is there: the end-of-year report showing how many ministries have been assisted through their little congregation.

We really like this idea and encourage other fellowships to follow suit. Of course you would have to arrive at your own priority statements and budget percentages; the principle to learn from the Los Angeles church is that your desire for mission must come *first*.

If you choose to establish this kind of fund, we'd like to suggest a few priorities for the money:

☐ Third World mission leaders. These people are leading the way in global mission, and it is wise, in our opinion, to fund their unique efforts. See our list in the "Resources" section. A dollar invested here goes a long way.

☐ Student mission education. Send your own youth to events that will build their global awareness and steer them toward a life of mission. We have listed several conferences for your consideration. You may also want to provide scholarships for formal education that has a mission emphasis.

☐ Inner-city education. How about taking on the challenge of our nation's crying need for quality education? Perhaps you could fund an entire year of special education for a local school program. Or if an urban Christian school is struggling to pay its teachers' modest salaries, you could cover a portion of one salary. It's a great feeling to know you have an emissary helping those children have a chance in life and demonstrating to them the love of Christ on your behalf.

☐ Industry. Mission is a wholistic enterprise. Several organizations are being formed that create industry at the local level—small businesses which create jobs, generate funds and provide education. These efforts are innovative and in need of some forward-looking supporters. A church in Philadelphia created a laundromat in a poorer district of the city. It is staffed with Christians from their church. This laundromat not only generates money for their ministry but also helps the church make natural contact with the locals.

32

Business and Mission

· · · · · · · · · · · ·

A farmer in a small rural community in the Northwest willed a couple hundred acres of his land to a church upon his death. The stipulation: all the proceeds of the land were to go into a mission fund.

Farmers divide up the responsibility of working the land. All labor and equipment is donated. And once a year a church picnic is held to commit the proceeds of the land to God's world. After lunch a convoy of combines and trucks moves onto the wheat field and gobbles up the grain. The imagery of bringing in the sheaves is not lost to these Christians.

All the funds are managed by a mission committee. People from all over the United States and the world apply to this little committee for financial support. The word is out. We think this is just about the best idea we have heard for funding mission. That one man has generated more for world outreach by his simple deed than most churches do.

We suggest that other churches follow the idea. If your church is in a rural community, there are ways to swap land and shift boundaries to create a special "endowed" property. If your fellowship has enterprising businesspeople, why not create a business that has the same goal? Most churches have retired members who would love to serve as volunteer staff at a company whose profits go entirely to world mission. Thrift shops, Christian gift and book stores and restaurants are just a few of the options you could pursue.

Set priorities as to who will receive the accumulated funds. Then form a church committee to oversee bookkeeping and disbursement. Throw an annual picnic or party at which you thank those who worked hard, announce how much money was given away, read thank-you letters from recipients and enjoy the blessing of giving.

33

Explore Community

· · · · · · · · · · · ·

One of the respondents to our research for this book urged us to call Christians toward "radical community." The case was made that we have not always placed a high priority on relationships, on the value of people over programs. In addition, we live in a fragmented national and international community where people seem more divided than at any previous time in our world history. Countries are disintegrating into mininations, empires are dismantling and communities are being ripped apart by groups demanding special treatment.

The gospel, at heart, is not an idea. It is the life of people who together follow Jesus. The life of sharing, caring for the weak, bearing one another's burdens, forgiving and reconciling is the hardest work of being Christian. But it is the essence. All of our lofty plans, massive organizations and public imaging as ministries are eventually going to go the way of wood, hay and stubble. We will be left with the gold nuggets of life lived in relationship, integrity, love. Many times we are drawn by this vision of the kingdom—we commit ourselves to work full time with Christian ministries because we believe in the substance of the gospel. But then problems emerge—coworkers are unloving, budget supersedes staffing, leaders are aloof and overly busy. What we thought was going to be an encounter with heaven is another trip through corporate America.

These experiences can be severely disillusioning. We are tempted to spew forth our righteous judgments on these groups and walk away, shaking the dust off our feet. Perhaps we have missed the point of community. It is in the crucible of relationships—where people normally give up on each other—that radical Christian community kicks in. It is here that we begin to wrestle with the temptation to exert our power as leaders (or as financiers), to make our moral pronouncements, to control our area of responsibility like a child, arms wrapped around toys, who screams, "Mine!"

The world will be won to Christ through the hard work of Christians who decide to love each other.

If you are interested in exploring radical Christian community through the life of intentional communities, you are in for a treat. We have listed several Christian communities in the "Resources" section. Take a summer to visit several of them. This is particularly feasible for college students and can forge some values that will last a lifetime.

Section

3

Careers in Missions

. . . .

34
Pioneer
· · · · · · · · · · ·

There are many parts of the world where the name of Jesus is still largely unknown. There is the need for Christians to take on the specific job of going "where no missionary has gone before." This is perhaps the most challenging of all mission assignments. We enter a world that is foreign to us in just about every aspect. Here is where these needs are most prominent today:

☐ Islam. This is the world's fastest-growing religion. And with its growth comes a culture of resistance to any outside influences that would threaten its sovereignty over people. Strong governments with heavy controls and censorship, prominent religious leaders who run their communities, and fringe military groups who feel called by Allah—these make for a terrible force.

Unfortunately, the West has perpetuated racist images of Muslims, and this has stalled opportunities to build bridges of love and friendship. There are close to one billion Muslims in the world today.

☐ Tribal animism. Throughout Africa, Asia and Latin America, animism is the chief religion. It may adopt certain Protestant, Catholic, Buddhist or Hindu elements, but basically it is a religion created out of the tribes' history of myths. Working in these regions often requires travel to remote and lonely places. Disease can attack missionaries, sometimes with lifetime effects; children are often separated from parents for educational reasons. Perhaps as many as one billion people live in these groups.

☐ Literacy training. The Bible has been partially translated into nineteen hundred languages. Large missions such as Wycliffe Bible Translators have developed teams of professionals who are likely to finish the job of making the Word of God available in all the world's languages. The Bible is now available to ninety-seven percent of the world's population. But the problem is that half the world's adults are illiterate. That's one-and-a-half billion people. The Bible is useless paper to them. Mission organizations are catching on to this vision, but their efforts are woefully understaffed and funded. Working in the area of literacy training can take you to virtually any spot of the globe and will put you in company as diverse as national presidents and country peasants. In the back of the book we have listed some groups you can contact for help.

35
Urban Ministry
· · · · · · · · · · · ·

Much of the world is migrating to the urban centers.
Whereas in the early 1800s just a few million people lived in
cities, today that total is closer to three billion. Cities are growing at such a rapid pace that the structures are just unable to
support the newcomers. Inadequate industry, housing, education, medicine, transportation, potable water and sanitary services lead to the crippling conditions we have learned to associate
with the inner city. Human suffering is off the charts. Crime and
gang life thrive in the vacuum of dignity, provision and protec-
tion.

The church, unfortunately, has often abandoned the city for the suburbs or country. The rationale has sometimes been to escape the corrupting influence that is "sure to lead us all to hell." Other times, the motive has been just plain fear.

God may guide some people away from these centers of pain, that is true. But we do not believe it should be the pattern of the church to walk away from human suffering. That is to be expected of secular people who do not have a relationship with the Lord of love and mercy. We, on the other hand, are called to follow the example of Christ, who looked out over the city of Jerusalem and wept.

Ministry to the city can take lots of forms. Some Christians have begun to move to the city simply to become a presence. No big ministry goals—just the daily life of salt and light. Their prayer has been that God will open specific opportunities to them in time. This more natural way of developing relationships with neighbors removes the label of "people who have come to preach to us." Others have formed industries that revitalize impoverished zones, worked with government to rework unjust laws that put burdens on the poor (housing, health, education and work laws), or established centers in the city that offer everything from schooling to legal counsel, recreation, tutoring, church and job skills training.

You are not alone if you decide to pursue a career in urban ministry. We have listed some organizations for you in the "Resources" section. If you believe God is guiding you to a future in the city, we recommend that you begin to take small steps in that direction. Begin to attend an inner-city church, do an internship there if you are a college or seminary student, relocate for a summer to a ministry that is making an impact for Jesus, get together with friends to rent an apartment in the city and attend seminars that will give you more information on how to become involved there.

Think of this as a long-term decision, and be patient with the process as God gives you opportunity to touch urban pain.

36
Tentmaking
. . . .

We mentioned earlier in this book that Christians are
warming up to the idea of a professional detour—an international stint, ranging from a couple of months to a couple of years,
that uses their vocational skills.

You may want to make a career out of this idea. The official
term for it is "tentmaker," borrowed from the apostle Paul who
supported his church-planting ministry in part by sewing tents.
The primary benefits of this form of career mission are:

☐ You do not enter another society in an unnatural form. People do not understand the traditional missionary. "Why do they
not work?" "Where do they get their money?" "Will I not have
to work if I follow their religion?" Tentmakers are people who
moved next door because they liked the job opportunity and are

attracted to the idea of living in another country. People understand that.

☐ Tentmaking also equalizes relationships. Instead of "I'm here on someone's dole to help you get your life fixed up," it's a matter of neighbors, who have mutually cranky bosses, trying to make a living and trying to build friendships.

☐ Tentmaking will get you into certain countries where traditional missionaries are barred from entry. Most nations welcome skills that will boost their economies or improve their educational systems.

☐ Tentmaking pays the way for your missionary service. Families that assume a more traditional approach to mission are often weighed down by the need to raise thousands of dollars in support for their living and ministry expenses. Missionaries sometimes feel reduced to beggars and resent the paternalistic relationship with churches that support them.

Some entrepreneurs have opted for a slightly different model to tentmaking—they start their own international businesses. These range from export-import to engineering consulting services to educational contracts. Creativity and service are the secrets of this approach. A successful business can free up additional time for you to interact with the business community and neighbors in the country where you have located.

See the "Resources" section for help in tentmaking.

37

Discipling Ministry

. . . .

The college years are crucial in their impact on our basic worldview. For most of us, this is the first opportunity to formulate our personal convictions. Up to now we were living off our parents' religion. In the environment of independence and pluralistic interaction, we are left alone to decide how we, personally, will follow Christ.

These important years give us the opportunity not only to make our faith personal but also to explore the world in a way our upbringing didn't allow. The college years are wonderful ones in this regard. Students have a host of options for traveling to the inner city, into Third World villages, across racial barriers, into drought territories and through secularized Europe. Stimuli send crashing messages from every side, and the idealistic, energetic college student may be more willing to explore God's heart for the world during these days than at any other period of life. Old paradigms of belief are challenged; new ones are willingly embraced.

It is for those at this unique stage of life that we urge people who are *beyond* student years to consider a career in discipling. If you have a desire to see thousands more Christians connect with God's call to the world, put yourself in the strategic spot of influencing students during those questioning years.

There are several ways to follow through on this idea:

☐ Contact a campus organization such as InterVarsity Christian Fellowship or Navigators, and ask how you can help as a volunteer.

☐ Join a church staff that is looking for a college sponsor. You'll be given carte blanche for involvement with college youth attending your church.

☐ Inquire about your denomination's campus ministry. Some of these have salaried posts for full-time college pastors. If your denomination does not have such a salaried post but would be willing to support you administratively, talk with your own pastor about getting help to raise your own salary.

☐ Join the residential staff of a Christian college. These posts put you full-time alongside the students you want to influence.

☐ Become a professor. This works well at either a secular university or a Christian college. Students are attracted to teachers who exhibit motivation for the subject, display an interest in students and seem connected to the international scene. Your influence can slowly grow to the point where you are helping students think through their call to the world.

38

Community Development

· · · · · · · · · · · ·

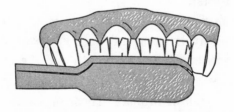

Christianity is good for the world in all aspects. We wor-
ship a Lord who created all of life and who looks tenderly upon
the suffering of society. Countless Scripture passages (inspired
through the Holy Spirit) call us to engage society at all levels
of suffering. We can be bold about our identity as Christ's family.

Christian community development is that discipline that asks
how the gospel will leave its fingerprints on a local community.
The question is wholesome—it looks at every aspect of life:
education, employment, safety, recreation, health, religion, family, transportation, toxic waste, water and much more. Several

opportunities are available to a Christian who wants to pursue this line of work as a serious professional. Governments and nongovernmental organizations alike are looking for people to move away from home to apply these skills. Training at a good secular university is a must if you choose to go this route. Schools like UCLA offer first-rate programs.

If you are considering a community development career in a Christian organization, you may want to do part of your studies in a Christian graduate program that is leading the way in thinking through this area. A place like Eastern College would be a great place to start.

And you may be able to contribute your specific skill to a larger community development effort. For example, hundreds of Christian dentists volunteer a month out of each year to work on people's teeth in regions where a concerted community development program is in place. Those organizations could not support full-time dentistry staff. The dentists do not desire to relocate on a full-time basis. The formula works well. Many eye doctors do the same thing.

Whatever path you choose to pursue in community development, we suggest that you build several crosscultural trips into your educational program. The more opportunities you have to explore other environments, the better your understanding of how community development works. (And those internships look great on your résumé.)

39
Administrative Posts

· · · · · · · · · · · ·

The work of Christ requires the whole body of Christ.
That is not our idea—it comes straight out of the Scriptures.

Relocating to distant and exotic places has a natural appeal to certain personality types. Commitment to mission for some may be a perfect fit for the kinds of creative gifts God gave them. But others are just not attracted to that kind of service. Does that mean they are excluded from the missionary task?

Definitely not. The truth is, most mission work is that—work. No matter what gifts you bring to the cause, you will be employing them with much sweat. And all the sweat gifts are needed.

Mission agencies are sometimes frustrated by the lack of interest in the administrative side of mission work. An enormous amount of machinery "drives" the process of getting the individual missionaries to the field and nurturing them and their ministries. That machinery requires accountants, truck drivers, typists, mechanics, organizers, builders, writers, software specialists, artists, architects, telephone operators and much more. The missionary cause often suffers because people who didn't qualify as evangelists or linguists stayed behind rather than exploring the support services.

We want to encourage people to actively approach the idea of administrative service as the unique contribution they can bring to mission. Contact mission organizations and tell them of your interest. Most of them would be happy to take you through the interview stage and recommend what kind of training you will need to be an expert member of the administrative staff. As other missionaries do, you will need to go through the process of determining whether or not the other areas of your life and Christianity are compatible—doctrinal positions, church history and family circumstances. And you will also need to choose between organizations that pay administrative staff a salary and those that require all staff to raise their own support.

These administrative positions may be in a home office or overseas. You may prefer one or the other—or sometimes it's possible to do both, on an occasional or rotating basis. Don't eliminate this unique mission opening until you've explored it a bit!

40
Teach
Mission

· · · · · · · · · · · ·

If you have spent several years in mission work and have a natural gift of teaching, consider the value of becoming a "mission professor." Not necessarily a person who teaches directly on the subject of mission, but one who brings the globe into the classroom and helps people think through their calling to the international scene.

There is a great need for sharp, fun, visionary professors in the college and seminary system. We need people who have been around the world a good number of times, who have lived in crosscultural settings for significant stretches, who have been exposed to a wide continuum of human need and have had to struggle with the relevance of their Christianity in today's world. These people can make pretty exciting teachers.

If you sense God may be calling you into this kind of career, here are a few pointers:

☐ Get the so-called terminal degree—the Ph.D. You do not want your credentials challenged just because you are raising difficult questions in the classroom.

☐ Get a range of crosscultural experiences that introduce you to church planting, development, justice, partnership and education.

☐ We strongly recommend that you include a Third World school as part of your educational track. Bring into your education the issues of people outside our culture.

☐ Choose a discipline that fits your training, experience and gifts. We would like to see globally minded professors make it into the entire catalog of college positions—economics, politics, literature, art, sociology, psychology and history, to name a few.

The Christian mission takes us to every level and every corner of society. We must not fall into the trap of encouraging global-minded Christians solely toward "religious" vocations. The university becomes a hotbed of activism—a great place for professors, administrators and students alike who are asking how they might bring all of society under the wing of God's love.

41
The
Pastorate
· · · · · · · · · · · ·

Pastors set the agendas for more than 350,000 congre-gations across the United States alone. That's a lot of influence.

And who are these pastors? They are ordinary people like you and me. They have hopes, disappointments, failures and successes. They struggle to use their strengths well, and they suffer quietly with their weaknesses. Does the list sound familiar? Like looking in the mirror? That's the point. Pastors are as human as the rest of us and yet they have a position of privilege and power.

If you have both a call to mission and a strong pastoral heart, we strongly urge you to consider the value of becoming a pastor. Mission depends on churches which have a healthy concern for the world, which are led by men and women who have a strong commitment to seeing the nations discipled. Going "over there" is not necessarily the natural or best way to work for the Great Commissioner.

If you would like to take this approach, we have a few suggestions:

☐ Get a good college degree that incorporates several trips abroad. Your plan must be to begin enlarging your own sense of how vast the world is. Be sure to include the spectrum of human need in those trips.

☐ Try to arrange an internship for a year or two under the leadership of a national pastor in a Third World setting. This will give you the chance to build bridges with the kinds of people who will be the future leaders of world mission. You begin to see the world from their perspective.

☐ You may also want to secure a one-year internship abroad with a mission organization. This offers you the unique perspective of what it is like to go through the application process and to live abroad in the mission community.

☐ Pursue a seminary education that includes a good mix of pastoral and mission concerns. You want to sharpen your skills in both of these areas.

☐ Try to secure a seminary internship that places you in an urban ethnic community.

Once you have your formal credentials and are looking for a place to serve, take a long view of the process. You are not trying to become the super-pastor of a super-mission church. You are looking for God to bring together your dual interest of pastoring and mission. You want to serve people at the point of their real needs and you want to point them to a world that calls for their compassionate response.

42
Post-Christian Countries

· · · · · · · · · · · ·

It is not a happy thought that whole countries have moved through the process of (1) being unevangelized to (2) experiencing the good news and embracing the message for themselves to (3) abandoning that message for a modern paradigm that does not allow the transcendent to impinge on reason. This is truly a tragic ending to a story of grace.

There are some Christians who have a special sensitivity to these nations. They have a love for the modern Western expressions of art and fashion, they are personally empathetic with many of the questions felt by citizens of post-Christian societies, and they understand the histories that have moved societies in that direction.

We believe God is calling uniquely qualified people into this form of service in the world mission of the church. And this ministry is not so much to call people back to their religion of old, but rather to call the religion of old forward to answer the contemporary questions.

Here are some of the specifics you may want to consider if this is your call:

☐ Look for a degree program that is well respected among post-modern academicians. You'll need to consider the top academic schools in several countries. The idea is to tap into a source of education that is directly connected to the story of the people with whom you plan to work.

☐ Take in the art, poetry, drama and music of the cultures to which you will speak. Include the whole spectrum of material as it spans the past several hundred years.

☐ Seek internships and study fellowships in European centers where some of the classical Enlightenment questions were raised.

☐ Spend at least a year in a European seminary to study the Reformation and the history of the expansion of the church.

☐ Develop the discipline of reading the great philosophical thinkers. Try to live inside the issues that hounded them to the pen.

☐ Practice the art of writing. This may be a unique gift of God and could become a means to enter the debate. Articles in prestigious journals can have significant impact on cultural waves of thought.

At the vocational level you will need to be creative. Options include joining a pastoral team, teaching in a Bible school or university, taking a national government assignment or diplomatic post, working in business and joining a traditional mission structure.

43
Domestic Service

· · · · · · · · · · · ·

Our final suggestion in the career section is simple
enough. We want to encourage you to think of mission opportunities in North America. Our society is terribly ravaged by
homelessness, unemployment, crime, illiteracy, ethnic division,
abuse of many sorts and a sense of little future. This should
amaze us when we think of all the full-time Christian workers
in the United States alone—one million of them.

Something is amiss. We believe that God is going to bring a
fresh day to the continent, that we will see fulfillment of the
prophecy of dead bones living and streams of living water flow-

ing. But we cannot see that this will happen through the channels of business as usual.

We pray that God will give young men and young women visions for this tired land. We pray that they will have the grace and courage to link together in a unified effort to seek the welfare of our nation. Their lives will incarnate the biblical call to love, service, hope and faith. We will find them in hospices, AIDS centers, convalescent homes, on gang turf, in the tenement buildings and on their knees. These will be the new missionaries of North America.

If God is stirring these kinds of thoughts in your heart, we encourage you to seek a covenant group of friends who will walk with you through this vision. Pray much together. Take corporate steps of faith. Visit communities that are walking a bold new path toward this kind of future. Learn from them and launch out into the terrifying, wonderful territory of pioneering in your own back yard.

Section
4

Resances
for Mission

• • • • • • • • • • • • • • • •

44

Service Agencies

. . . .

There are several mission groups that do not take missionaries. Their job is to provide a special service to the mission movement. We have referred to these different groups throughout the book. Here is a list of organizations that will help you implement many of the ideas we have suggested.

ACMC
(helps church mission
committees)
P. O. Box ACMC
Wheaton, IL 60189

Adopt-A-People
(helps you do just that)
1605 Elizabeth Street
Pasadena, CA 91104

AIMS
(helps charismatic churches
do mission)
P. O. Box 64534
Virginia Beach, VA 23464

Alternative Gift Markets, Inc.
(a nonprofit ministry which
sends to the needy the gift
you sponsor in a friend's
name—twenty seedlings to a
reforestation project in the
Dominican Republic for $10,
for example, or one goat for
$37 to provide milk and
meat for protein-deficient
children in Indonesia—and
then sends your friend an attractive card announcing the
gift sent in his or her honor)
9656 Palomar Trail
Lucerne Valley, CA 92356

BridgeBuilders
(helps you put together your
short-term trip; a full-service
agency)
9925 7th Way N. #102
St. Petersburg, FL 33702

Discover the World
(helps train you for a quality
short-term mission)
3255 E. Orange Grove Blvd.
Pasadena, CA 91107

Harvest International
(helps you twin with other
churches)
1979 E. Broadway, #2
Tempe, AZ 85282

Martin International
(a full-service travel agency
focused on the needs of
short-term mission)
8219 Denver St.
Ventura, CA 93004

45
Mission
Seminars

· · · · · · · · · · ·

Some of these groups have a seminar all set to go; others want to work with you to tailor a seminar to fit your needs. These organizations are also storehouses of information. They would be willing to help you with a lot more than hosting a seminar.

Bread for the World
802 Rhode Island Ave., NE
Washington, DC 20018

Discover the World
(see previous page)

Destination 2000
1610 Elizabeth Street
Pasadena, CA 91104

Evangelicals for Social
 Action
10 Lancaster Avenue
Wynnewood, PA 19151

Zwemer Muslim Institute
P.O. Box 365
Altadena, CA 91001

46
Conferences

· · · · · · · · · · · ·

Conferences are primarily a resource: a place to pick up new ideas and an annual opportunity to renew friendships with people who are pursuing the same ideas you are.

ACMC
(church-related—usually
held in early summer)
P.O. Box ACMC
Wheaton, IL 60189

AIMS
(charismatic, church-
related—usually held in
the spring)
P.O. Box 64534
Virginia Beach, VA 23464

Christian Community Development Association
(leaders' meeting—held in the spring)
P.O. Box 459
Angeles Camp, CA 95221

EFMA
(mission leaders of more than ninety organizations—held in the fall)
1023 15th St. NW, Suite 500
Washington, DC 20005

ISFM
(mission leaders focusing on Unreached Peoples—held in the fall)
1605 Elizabeth St.
Pasadena, CA 91104

Miami Conference
(designed for people sponsoring short-term mission teams—held in late January)
P.O. Box 52-7900
Miami, FL 33152

SCUPE
(designed for people in urban ministry—held in the spring)
30 W. Chicago Ave.
Chicago, IL 60610

Urbana
(nation's largest student mission convention—held every three years over Christmas break)
c/o InterVarsity Christian Fellowship
P.O. Box 7895
Madison, WI 53707-7895

47
Other
Organizations

We have already listed several organizations ready to help you in your mission vision. We mentioned a few other groups in this book, and we list their addresses below.

Domestic Ministries:

EAPE
(Tony Campolo)
P.O. Box 238
St. Davids, PA 19087

Harambee Family Center
(John Perkins)
1581 Navarro Ave.
Pasadena, CA 91103

Mendenhall Ministries
(rural)
309 Center St.
Mendenhall, MS 39114

Intentional Christian Communities:

Jesus People USA
920 W. Wilson Ave.
Chicago, IL 60640

Sojourners Community
P. O. Box 29272
Washington, DC 20017

Third World Ministries:

Ajith Fernando
Youth For Christ
P. O. Box 1311
Colombo
SRI LANKA

Vishal Mangalwadi
105 Savitri Commercial
Complex
Greater Kailash II
New Delhi 110048
INDIA

Caesar Molebatsi
Youth Alive Ministries
P.O. Box 129
Soweto
REPUBLIC OF SOUTH
AFRICA

Pedro Arana
Misión Urbana y Rural
Apartado 21-0005
Lima 21
PERU

48

Magazines, Newsletters, Journals

· · · · · · · · · · ·

Context
Published by World Vision
Canada, gives insightful
looks at Canadian culture
and church.
Quarterly, free
6630 Turner Valley Rd.
Mississauga, Ontario
L5N 2S4
CANADA

PRISM
A new, national magazine
calling the church to work
for global evangelism and social transformation.
Monthly, $25.00
10 Lancaster Ave.
Wynnewood, PA 19096

Evangelical Missions Quarterly
Published by the mission leaders of EFMA—a journal of current issues that touch missionaries.
Quarterly, $17.95
P.O. Box 794
Wheaton, IL 60189

International Bulletin of Missionary Research
Published by the Overseas Ministry Study Center—covers the broad range of mission issues in the evangelical-conciliar-Catholic debate.
Quarterly, $18.00
P.O. Box 3000
Denville, NJ 07834

MARC Newsletter
Published by World Vision International—gives the latest news, information and resources on world mission.
Quarterly, free
919 West Huntington Dr.
Monrovia, CA 91016

Ministry Currents
Published by Barna Research Group, focuses on ways to improve your church outreach.
Quarterly, $20.00
722 West Broadway
Glendale, CA 91204

Together Journal
Published by World Vision International—the best current look on Christian community development.
Quarterly, $12.00
919 West Huntington Dr.
Monrovia, CA 91016

Transformation Journal
Published by a coalition of international evangelical leaders—a dialogue on mission and ethics.
Quarterly, $24.00
P.O. Box 11127
Birmingham, AL 35202

Urban Family
Published by the Perkins Foundation—the magazine

of hope and progress for African-American families.
Quarterly, $11.80
P.O. Box 40125
Pasadena, CA 91104

WorldWatch
Published by the World-Watch Institute—a secular group that has earned the reputation of leading the way in issues of poverty and environment.
Bimonthly, $15.00
1776 Massachusetts Ave. N.W.
Washington, DC 20036

49
Books

· · · · · · · · · · · ·

Reference Books

Amnesty International Report. New York: Amnesty International, 1993. Published annually.

Brown, Lester, et al., eds. *State of the World.* Washington, D.C.: WorldWatch Institute, 1993. Published annually.

Jansen, Frank Kaleb, ed. *Target Earth.* Pasadena, Calif.: Global Mapping Project, 1989.

Roberts, Dayton, ed. *Mission Handbook: North American Protestant Ministries Overseas.* 15th ed. Pasadena, Calif.: MARC, 1993.

Simon, Art, ed. *State of the Hungry World.* Washington, D.C.: Bread for the World, 1993. Published annually.

Short-Term Mission Resources

Aeschliman, Gordon, ed. *Short-Term Mission Handbook.* Evanston, Ill.: Berry Publishing Services, 1992. Phone (708) 869-1573.

Burns, Ridge, and Noel Becchetti. *The Complete Student Missions Handbook.* Grand Rapids, Mich.: Zondervan, 1990.

Eaton, Chris, and Kim Hurst. *Vacations with a Purpose: A Planning Handbook for Your Short-Term Missions Team.* Colorado Springs: NavPress, 1991.

Gibson, Tim, et al., eds. *Stepping Out.* Seattle, Wash.: YWAM Publishing, 1992.

Millham, Jacquelyn. *Discoveries Reflection Notebook.* Pasadena, Calif.: Discover the World, 1990. Phone (818) 577-9502.

Peterson, Roger. *Is Short-Term Really Worth the Time and Money?* Minneapolis: STEM, 1991. Phone (612) 535-2944.

General Mission Books

Aeschliman, Gordon. *GlobalTrends.* Downers Grove, Ill.: IVP, 1990.

Bakke, Ray. *The Urban Christian.* Downers Grove, Ill.: IVP, 1987.

Borthwick, Paul. *How to Be a World-Class Christian.* Wheaton, Ill.: Victor Books, 1990.

_____. *A Mind for Missions.* Colorado Springs: NavPress, 1989.

Bryant, David. *In the Gap.* Ventura, Calif.: Regal Books, 1984.

Campolo, Tony. *The Kingdom of God Is a Party.* Dallas: Word, 1991.

_____. *Wake Up America!* San Francisco: HarperSanFrancisco, 1991.

Costas, Orlando. *Liberating News*. Grand Rapids, Mich.: Eerdmans, 1989.

Hayner, Stephen, and Gordon Aeschliman, eds. Global Issues Bible Studies. Downers Grove, Ill.: IVP, 1990.

Johnstone, Patrick. *Operation World*. Atlanta, Ga.: STL, 1989.

Lovelace, Richard. *Renewal As a Way of Life*. Downers Grove, Ill.: IVP, 1985. Out of print; check with your pastor or church library.

Newbigin, Lesslie. *The Gospel in a Pluralistic Society*. Grand Rapids, Mich.: Eerdmans, 1989.

Perkins, John. *Beyond Charity*. Grand Rapids, Mich.: Baker Books, 1993.

Richardson, Don. *Peace Child*. Ventura, Calif.: Regal Books, 1974.

Tucker, Ruth. *From Jerusalem to Irian Jaya*. Grand Rapids, Mich.: Zondervan, 1983.

50
Videos
• • • • • • • • • • •

Concerts of Prayer
Single video narrated by David Bryant on spiritual awakening and world mission. Published by Regal Books, Ventura, CA 93003

Cry Justice
Single video narrated by John Perkins regarding urban need. Published by Regal Books, Ventura, CA 93003

Destination 2000
Five videos on church planting. Published by Frontiers, 1610 Elizabeth St., Pasadena, CA 91104

The City for God's Sake
Three videos on urban mission. Published by Regal Books, Ventura, CA 93003

The Search
An exploration of New Age issues. Published by 2100 Productions, P.O. Box 7895, Madison, WI 53707-7895